# TAKE YOUR
# SHOT

### HOW TO GROW YOUR BUSINESS, ATTRACT MORE CLIENTS, AND MAKE MORE MONEY

# ROBIN WAITE
## BESTSELLING AUTHOR OF ONLINE BUSINESS STARTUP

First Published in Great Britain 2017

By Robin M. Waite

ISBN 978-0-9957768-0-7

Robin Waite Limited
Stroud House
Russell Street
Stroud
Gloucestershire
GL5 3AN

www.robinwaite.com

# PRAISE

"Take Your Shot is a great, easy-to-read book that contains some serious messages for anyone working hard at building a business. I came across a phrase many years ago which can apply to many self-employed individuals "it's easy to become a busy fool". Reading this book will stop you falling into that trap as the serious messages are about the importance of belief, aiming high, being brave creating systems and surrounding yourself with the right people. A very uplifting read as the reader follows the journey of the main character as he learns to work smarter and enjoy life again."

**Sandra Webber, High-Performance Coach and Author of *Own It - Regain Control and Live Life on Your Terms***

"Robin's book is so much better than the usual 'how to' publication. By telling a story based on a real business owner, he takes us on a journey that will resonate with readers no matter what industry they are in, no matter how small or large their enterprise.

The main character has a wise coach, David, who reminds us all to look at our business, not as it is but as it can be. If you are one of those business owners is always 'busy', this book will help you to investigate what you are busy doing and whether you are effectively working towards a goal that truly motivates you.

With a step by step approach that is easy to understand and implement, if you do what the book suggests, you will achieve the outstanding success you deserve."

**David Tovey, Business Owner, Speaker and Author of *Principled Selling – How to Win More Business Without Selling Your Soul.***

"What a book. Robin is a business coach extraordinaire and a fantastic human being, but he has outdone himself with this piece of genius. Unlike most business help books, this reads like a novel you can't put down. This isn't because it's crazy and out of this world, but instead because he describes the thoughts and actions of every business owner at their start or point of frustration in their business. The special thing about Robin and this book is that he looks at the business owner, not the business. He brings you on a journey where you can't help but have lightbulb moments. The only thing better for your business than this book is working with the man himself."

**Michael Serwa - Coach for the Elite (michaelserwa.com)**

"Well... Robin has smashed it out the park (or off the green, if you prefer!) with his second book. It's a relatable story, which I'm sure will resonate with everyone. What I love is that Robin has picked out the key learnings about pricing and productisation, and weaved them into the story so that everyone can benefit. Fantastic."

**Carl Reader - Author of The Startup Coach,**
**Multiple Business Owner, and Serial Entrepreneur**

"Storytelling at its finest! Take your shot packs a positive punch which will help entrepreneurs in any industry to reassess their goals. We hear the painful, lonely tale from the perspective of Robin's golf pro whose business is unrewarding and feel his struggle in his everyday life. Then the kickass teaching begins, where Robin adeptly describes key steps of the journey as the coach helps him re-design a set of products which people want, not that they need. This book highlights how businesses can offer value in unique ways for their customers and achieve success on their terms. An inspiring transformation story, which every business owner should read."

**Daniel Priestley- Entrepreneur and Author**

# CONTENTS

FOREWORD                                        1

INTRODUCTION                                    3

CHAPTER 1: BREAKING POINT                       7

CHAPTER 2: A CHANCE ENCOUNTER                  13

CHAPTER 3: THE FIRST LESSON                    21

CHAPTER 4: SET A GOAL                          29

CHAPTER 5: CREATE A PRODUCT                    39

CHAPTER 6: TAKE YOUR SHOT                      47

CHAPTER 7: MAKE MORE MONEY                     53

CHAPTER 8: SIGN ON THE DOTTED LINE             59

CHAPTER 9: WOW!                                67

CHAPTER 10: PIXIE DUST                         75

CHAPTER 11: FREEDOM                            83

CHAPTER 12: SUNSET                             89

NEXT STEPS                                     91

ABOUT THE AUTHOR                               93

FEARLESS BUSINESS                              96

READING LIST                                   97

For Charlotte, Poppy and Sophie

# FOREWORD

One roll of the dice.

That's all any of us get on this planet, whether you are religious, spiritual, atheist or haven't got a a f*cking clue.

Once your time here on earth is up?

It's up.

It took me a long time to realise this fact, and as 'morbid' as an introduction to this book as that may be? It's a fact. Plain and simple.

I felt it was apt for this book 'Take Your Shot' as that's what we have at life:

One shot.

Why would would want to live your life unhappy, unfulfilled and unable to help others (as well as yourself) achieve everything you want.

As someone who has 1000's of books, and two best sellers of my own I urge you not to just read this book, but take **ACTION**.

Right now you still draw breath and your heart still beats; coupled with the fact where we are at a time in civilisation where we have everything at our fingertips and - being blunt - no excuses NOT to make the changes and do the work that needs to be done.

So, I leave you with this.

You have every right to life the life you want - on your terms; yes there will be hard work and sacrifice - but not forever. Use this book, take action and reclaim your f*cking life, NOW.

**Dan Meredith – Bestselling Author of How to be F*cking Awesome and leader of Coffee With Dan**

# INTRODUCTION

*Take Your Shot* is the story about Russ Hibbert and his chance meeting with business coach, David. Russ is a hard worker, dedicated to his wife and children, and building a career as a golf professional.

Based on an early case study in my coaching career, *Take Your Shot*, tells the story of a consultation I held with a golf professional. It lasted only ten minutes and transformed my client's business and life.

I have coached many similar businesses to Russ's business. Over 250 in fact since 2004. From small boutique design agencies turning over £1,000 per month to large accountancy firms turning over £2m+ per year. From online directories to medical aesthetics businesses, and singing coaches to hospitality experts.

The common issue shared by all 250 business owners that I have worked with is that, at some point during their career, they have all faced challenges when growing their businesses.

Despite these challenges; each one of them runs a successful business, but the business owner realises that there is an opportunity for their business to grow further. The owner is frustrated at throwing all of their time and energy into their business but not experiencing significant growth. Their families are getting frustrated that they don't see their partner, father, husband or wife as much as they would like to. Life for my clients isn't a struggle, but they want to get a piece of their life back.

I want to share this story with you now to save you the hassle of facing the same challenges and allow you to accelerate the growth of your business.

This book is for any service based business owner at any stage in business. It is for anyone who has lost their way in business and can't understand why they go from week-to-week ending up at the same place every single Sunday evening. It is designed to get you out of your own way so you can focus *ON* your business.

I coach the business owner, and not the business. I spent 16 years figuring out all of the tough stuff so that my clients don't have to and I've encapsulated my most important learnings into *Take Your Shot*.

Typically businesses I work with double their turnover in as little as three months. If you implement some of the tips, I offer in *Take Your Shot* I can guarantee that you will start to see long lasting results in the next three to six months.

I hope that *Take Your Shot* inspires you to take action, re-evaluate your product offering, tweak your pricing, focus on getting serious clients on board who are committed to making positive changes, and understand what value you are offering.

*Take Your Shot* is not for someone looking for a 'get rich quick scheme' or 'quick wins'. *Take Your Shot* does not offer immediate results. Business change and growth requires work, commitment, and most importantly the balls and an open mind to make incredibly bold, brave decisions.

*Take Your Shot* is not 'the answer'. But, it is designed to inspire you into taking action and doing things differently in your business.

If you want to be pushed outside of your comfort zone and to take the next big leap in your business, then I invite you to read on.

The early chapters set the scene and uncover the mindset issues Russ is suffering around his business and how these impact upon his personal life. Russ then learns how goals help to create clarity and focus. Chapters 5, 6 & 7 introduce three core areas of business; Product, Pricing, and Value Propositions.

And then finally Russ learns some very important lessons about sales. Get the offer right, and you can charge what you want for your products and services, not what everyone else is charging. Sales become effortless.

Follow the simple steps in *Take Your Shot*, and I can guarantee you will change the perceptions of your own business. I hope that it will give you a more positive mindset around what is achievable in business. If you're in a bit of a fog in your business, prepare for the landscape to become incredibly clear again.

**How to use this book:**

Read it all, and see whether there are any similarities between yours' and Russ' businesses.

Pushed for time? Then look out for David's Lessons as indicated by the grey boxes and Russ's Lightbulb moments as noted by the light bulb icon to the right.

The models I use in this book represent examples of the tools I use in my coaching programme. Each tool includes a simple diagram, a short 5-10 minute explanation followed by a discussion between David and Russ about how Russ can implement the tool in his business.

If you have any questions please go to my website and to find out more about my Fearless Business Coaching programme:

http://robinwaite.com/fearless/application

**6** TAKE YOUR SHOT

# CHAPTER 1: BREAKING POINT

I stumbled out of bed into the darkness; it must have been about a quarter past five in the morning. I pulled the curtain back to see what the weather was doing, and I could see that there was a heavy frost on the cars parked in the cul de sac. Today was going to be a tough day.

The winter had set in already, despite it only being October. It's this time of year when I struggle with getting out of bed. The darkness was oppressive, and the dreariness of winter brought out absolute depression and anxiety in me.

I let the curtain fall back into place and fumbled my way around the end of the bed in what little light I could see.

THUMP!

"This bloody bed!" I muttered to myself under my breath, having just cracked my thigh on the corner of the bed for the third time this week.

I was more worried about waking up my wife, Susan, and our 11-month-old baby, Jacob, who was still sleeping in his crib in our bedroom.

My first daughter, Elena, had been fine; the sleep deprivation was bearable, and I'd been full of motivation having just started up my business working as a golf professional. But with Jacob, I struggled. The tiredness was unbearable and made me unbearable as a result.

As much as I loved coming home after a day at work; the transition between work brain and 'Daddy brain' was impossible. Shifting from a hectic day teaching, to rush hour traffic and then into the bath and bedtime routine was a nightmare.

I felt most sorry for Susan who, yet again for another night, had been up 2, 3 4, 6…8 times that night and not slept for any more than half an hour. I knew that she'd be seething in bed right now.

I had no choice and continued to fight my way through the darkness, switching on the fan above the door leading to the bathroom, and closing the door behind me. In the shower, I quietly contemplated my day ahead; remembering that I had a full book of 8 clients. My adrenaline started to pump, and my heart and brain raced with thoughts.

I was going to give this Saturday absolutely everything.

I finished my shower, did my hair, sprayed on some deodorant and brushed my teeth…and then my heart sank. I remembered that, yet again, I had to get dressed in the dark so not to wake Jacob up.

The cot was blocking my wardrobe door in our tiny bedroom. So, I scraped some clothes up off the floor. Making my way downstairs the hallway light lit the way and, passing the hallway mirror; I realised my shirt was not only on inside-out but also back-to-front. As I rushed to change my shirt round, I realised that I was already 10 minutes late…I grabbed an apple and filled my water bottle, scrabbled for my bag and keys and headed for the front door to begin my 1-hour commute to the course.

Rounding the corner onto the driveway, I spotted my car, heavily frosted. During the 5 minutes rushing around the car, frantically spraying de-icer and scraping ice off the windscreen with my credit card, I thought to myself, "I wish that one day I could get up at a sensible bloody time, and have breakfast with my family before going to work!"

As the car spluttered into life, I remembered that my spiked shoes were still inside; still dirty from yesterday having not had time to clean them the evening before. As I opened the door to the house, I could hear little Jacob stirring upstairs, and then Susan's heavy footsteps getting out of bed. I wanted to go and give her a hug and deal with Jacob so Susan could have a lie-in…but I was now late for work so I snuck quietly back out of the house.

------

I was supporting my family by way of the business; getting out there and getting my hands dirty earning money and working incredibly hard. I had sacrificed friendships and given up my own time. Most days I questioned whether it was worth it.

I'd barely had time to speak to Susan during the past week. I felt the only way to make more money was to offer more lessons, which meant I'd spent seven days solid on the golf course. Not only that, but the other pro had been off sick for three days, so I had to double up my lessons.

Having worked 13 days out of the last two weeks, had no real holiday to speak of in 6 months, and always struggling with money, I was considering jacking it in. Susan had tried to put some shopping on the joint account yesterday, and the payment declined. She was mortified and came home fuming that evening. She didn't speak to me at all, not even to say, "Good night!"

------

The traffic was heavier than normal. I could see the lights of the cars and the lorries stretching ahead, queuing up to the motorway. Thinking to myself, "I'm never going to get there on time?" my thoughts turned to the manager of the course, who would likely give me grief for being late. How is it possible to get up at 5 am and still be late for work? I could feel my anxiety levels rising.

My mind started to wonder, what if I had a regular job? It wouldn't be what I loved doing, but that's ok, right? What if I just had a normal job which paid me a regular salary, which is in my account every month?"

I could go to work at 9 am and leave work at 5 pm as everybody else does.

And then I remembered…

 I used to do that, and it was never nine to five. My boss always wanted another pound of flesh. Most days I was leaving at 7 am and not getting home until 7 pm.

It can't carry on like this. Me, doing the same thing day in day out but things weren't getting any better. I had to change something, now, but what?

Whether you work for yourself or someone else; whether you work in an office or outdoors; it makes absolutely no difference. My daydream had come full circle, and I realised I am one of the lucky few who gets to pursue my passion and do a job I love. Despite the fact some of my clients are an absolute pain in the backside, 80% of them are fantastic. Wouldn't it be great, I thought to myself if I could do something about that other 20%?

But what?

I had to turn up and hope the eight people who had booked lessons today were going to show up on time…or at all. Lo and behold I felt my heart sink as my phone buzzed twice and a text message arrived. Between 6 am and 7 am a message was from one of two people; Susan, wishing me luck for the day ahead, or one of my clients cancelling their lesson. The traffic was static, so I glanced at my iWatch and could see:

"Hey Russ, really sorry mate, can't make it. Hope that's not a problem. See you next week. Thanks, Jez."

Jeremy was my first client of the day…well, not anymore.

I had been looking forward to working with Jeremy. He had a good swing and didn't have a bad game. However, for the last three weeks, Jeremy had sent the same message cancelling his lesson at the last minute. Jeremy even booked the 7 am appointment so he could get a lesson in before work.

I collected payments after lessons; this meant I was already down £25 before getting into work. The arrangement I had signed with the owner of the course meant that I had to pay a fixed fee for each lesson booked, regardless of whether the client turned up, so this was now costing me money.

The main driving force behind setting up my own business was to help as many people as possible to improve their golf game, and making a difference in their lives. I know how much people love playing golf, being outdoors, and being able to take a break from their work and family. My clients need the time out to unwind from a stressful week.

Not only did I not know what to do about Jeremy not turning up, I knew that it would also reflect poorly on me. Jeremy would be out on the course with his friends, and his game wouldn't be improving. His friends would ask, "Jez, don't you have golf lessons? Your teacher can't be that good."

As I pulled the car onto the course; I could see a shimmer of frost and wondered what I was going to do for the next hour. Resigning myself to the fact that I would be spending the first hour of the day tidying the pro shop instead of delivering a lesson. Just like the last 3 Saturdays.

Another message pinged through on my phone; this time from Susan.

"Morning, my darling, hope you got into the office ok. Just wanted to let you know how much I love you and how proud I am for you sticking at this golf thing. Can't wait to see you later xx."

# CHAPTER 2: A CHANCE ENCOUNTER

I set about pricing the second-hand golf clubs that had been left muddled in an old cardboard box in the corner of the shop. The box hadn't moved in two weeks; not since Pete, the other golf pro had last attempted to price them.

"Pete, where's the list of these clubs?" I shouted across the shop.

Pete was in his mid-fifties, a full head of grey hair and a slightly bulging paunch, he seemed like he'd given up on life and hardly represented the sporting elite pictured on the TV.

There is a list where we write down the amount paid for each club, if anything at all, and the sale price to ensure we made a profit.

"I dunno mate!" Pete shouted back, "I put it in the box."

I had another quick look inside the box, "It's not there, Pete." The missing list meant I didn't know how much we'd paid for the clubs. I set about creating a new list and finding the prices of the clubs on sites like eBay and Gumtree to get a comparison. I added 20% on as we provided a 6-month guarantee with the clubs we sell.

I'd gone through three or four clubs when a gentleman walked into the shop. He wandered over to the gloves, and then over to the shoes. Smartly dressed in a pair of chinos and a Ralph Lauren polo shirt, a shiny pair of leather shoes…I'm sure I spotted a Gucci logo on them; I watched him sidle over to the woods near Pete, who was oblivious to the customer.

Eventually, I wandered over.

"Hi there, I'm Russ, is there anything I can help you with?"

The chap looked at me, "Yes, actually, there is. I'm interested in some lessons. I used to play a long time ago, and am thinking about taking it up again." I saw an opportunity, and blurted out the first thing I could think of, "How long have you got?"

He looked at me slightly bemused, "What…do you mean?"

"My lesson cancelled this morning, so if you've got the time now then why don't we head out onto the driving range and take a look at your swing?"

"Well, er, sure…ok!"

I gathered up some clubs that looked about the right size for my new client and shouted across to him, "What do you want to do? Irons? Wedges? Putting? Woods?"

"Irons?"

I led my potential client out onto the driving range and started in the same old way I always do with a new client. I neatly, and purposefully, laid ten golf balls down in a line on the floor of the bay that was going to be home for the next 45 minutes and offered him a three iron…damn, I hadn't even asked him what his name was yet, idiot.

"So, what's your name by the way? Apologies for not asking before in the shop." I asked.

"I'm David, pleased to meet you, Russ!" he said and offered me a confident handshake. "So, what's the plan?"

"Hit the balls," I said, "I want to have a look at your swing and see where your game is at."

David took his time and steadily worked his way along the line of balls, carefully adjusting his stance and grip with each swing.

The first shot he completely fluffed; the ball bounced along the ground like a stone skipping on water. David could sense himself tensing up, and took a deep intake of breath before the second shot. This time it sailed high into the air with a very slight slice on it, "Still got it!" he said calmly before preparing for his third swing, which he hooked carelessly left causing a couple of golfers in neighbouring bays to glance towards our bay.

And so it continued until David had sent all ten balls on their way. I assessed the situation; at least six had gone where David had intended them to go. He was a bit rusty, and his shoulders and back were stiff. It wouldn't take much to get his game back on the straight and narrow.

"How long ago did you play?" I asked David.

"I used to play when I was in my teens and twenties, but I got a job and got married, had kids and…well, I'm sure you've heard that story a thousand times? It's been 20 years or so since I last picked up a club in anger."

"What do you want to achieve through having lessons?" I asked.

"I just want to get a bit fitter again," David said, "And I've recovered a bit of time. I enjoy my golf, so thought I'd give it another go."

"Are you retired? How have you managed to recover some time?"

David went on to explain to me about how he was still working and, while busy, had managed to reduce his hours. When I stopped to ask him what he did, David paused, and took his time to tell me, "I'm a business coach."

I'd met a few business coaches in the past, but it's a career I know little about and never thought that I needed one. I gained a degree in Business Management with honours and felt that this furnished me with everything I needed to know when I started my business. I knew they earned good money, but that was about it.

"What does a business coach do?" I blurted out.

"Ah!" he said, "Most people do the same thing day in and day out, whether it be in a job or their own business. People are always  incredibly busy, and finances are tight. Life is constantly in a state of stress. But, if you just carry on doing the same old thing, nothing is ever going to change."

"It sounds like you're describing me!"

"Coaching is not for someone who isn't willing to take criticism. I coach the person and not the business, so the relationship I build with my clients is critical. If someone says, 'Yes, but…' to me; they are not coachable. You have to want to be coached. Otherwise, it never works."

"Ha!" I laughed, "That sounds like Pete!"

He went on, "I coach people, using a toolkit which I have developed, primarily around product architecture, pricing and value propositions." David could see a blank look come across my face, "I help business owners build a suite of products which build trust with their clients. I teach my clients how to build more value into their products meaning they can charge more than their competitors."

"I also teach my clients to spend more time with their prospects, so there is a greater chance of them understanding the full value of the product or service they are about to buy."

"I call this packaging," David explained, "It makes the sales process less complicated and the marketing message easier to communicate. If my clients execute the strategies we create, then they will earn more money and create time for themselves."

"I work on mindset, productivity and all sorts of other aspects of their business to ensure my clients stay active and have clear goals and objectives. Sorry! That was quite a long explanation, but did that make sense?"

I took stock and allowed it to sink in, "Do you know what I would give, right now, to get some time back? And some more money."

"Go on." David invited me to tell him more.

"Take today, I've just had a client cancel on me. I work from 7 am to 6 pm most days of the week. There's only ever two or three lessons booked but tonnes to do on the course. At the weekend it's eight or nine lessons back-to-back. When my wife goes back to work, we're not going to see each other." I took a deep breath, "I want to spend more time with her and the kids."

David replied without hesitation, "Tell me more. How old are your kids?"

"My eldest is coming up for seven, and the youngest is just 11 months old. We planned it of course, but it's full on. And Susan, my wife, is constantly stressed and tired. I don't see them most mornings or evenings because I'm here trying to get the business off the ground."

"I've got two daughters myself," David jumped in, "I mean they're grown up now. I remember those days like they were yesterday, rushing around, always busy…and exhausting!"

"Tell me about it!" I said, and we both chuckled in unison.

"But there's a funny energy you get when kids come into the mix. I managed to harness that energy and set up my coaching practice; it was the most productive I'd ever been. You can do anything, you know, Russ, when you put your mind to it."

I could feel my heart soar. I could tell David understood how I was feeling. He had an enormous warmth emanating from him. I couldn't quite put my finger on it, but I trusted him.

"What do you think?" David asked abruptly.

"Business coaching sounds great…"

"No, no! My swing, what do you think of my golf swing?"

"Sorry. It's brilliant actually; given you've not played in so long. You scored 6 out of 10 which means there is still a golfer in you. How do you feel about having some lessons?" I asked.

"I'd love some lessons, Russ, sounds like we could both learn from one another. How does it work?"

I explained to David that the lessons were £25 per hour and each client has the same time slot each week, so there are no excuses to miss lessons. Payment is taken at the end of the lesson, and all lessons are an hour. I wanted to demonstrate my flexibility by saying that lessons are guided by what my clients want to learn that week.

"When can I start?" David asked.

I don't know why, and emotions probably got the better of me, but very unprofessionally I announced to David, "The guy who's meant to be here now has had his third strike, he missed three lessons in a row. He's obviously not committed, so I now have an opening. How about Tuesday mornings at 7 am? Would that work for you?"

"That works just fine with me Russ, book me in."

The 45-minute lesson flew by and before I knew it the time was up. I collected up the clubs and left the balls to pick up during lunch. David and I walked towards the shop together. As it was only still 8 am the car park was relatively empty. I spotted this lovely black Range Rover. It was an Autobiography. I knew what it was because, pre-children, I'd spent time daydreaming and browsing the Land Rover website customising my Autobiography.

"Thank you so much for this morning, Russ, and for fitting me in like that." David said, offering his hand again for another bone shattering handshake, "I'm looking forward to my next lesson."

"Me too!" I said without thinking.

David jumped into the driver's seat, closed the door. The V8 roared into life. David leant out of the driver's side window, "Russell, get yourself a copy of Napoleon Hill's Think and Grow Rich. If you understand 'the secret' in it, you'll see that it is always possible to have more. But, you've got to know what 'more' looks like to you, and have an unyielding desire to achieve it."

With that, he reversed out of the space, and then set off up the driveway. I stood and watched it disappear out of the gates.

# CHAPTER 3: THE FIRST LESSON

I had a frustrating week after meeting David. Even before the weekend arrived, there were four cancellations. I chased Jeremy down and broke the news to him that I was cancelling his lessons due to missing three in a row. Needless to say, he hadn't taken it well, sworn profusely and finally put the phone down on me.

I woke up with a start early on Saturday morning and, as I scratched around for my phone, it dawned on me that it wasn't my alarm clock that had woken me up.

My phone lit up the room telling me that it was a little after 3 am, a whole two hours before my alarm was due to go off.

I could hear the rain tapping down loudly outside. Bloody rain.

When it rained, particularly in the weekend, work was a disaster. The worst I'd had was six cancellations out of eight lessons booked. That wasn't the worst part; that day, only the first and last clients turned up meaning I filled the entire day with cleaning out the stock room in the shop, cleaning the toilets, cleaning the kitchen and the stairs, and cleaning pretty much anything in flipping sight.

I couldn't drift back off to sleep. My mind spent two hours racing over numerous topics; the ensuing MOT on our old car, the cancellations in the week and the probable cancellations today, Susan's suggestion last night that I start looking for a job, and what sort of a world I was dragging my children up?

Eventually, my thoughts drifted onto something more positive. I reflected on what David said during his brief lesson earlier in the week. You can do anything you want to when you put your mind to it. So, I did. I dreamed about playing on the tour alongside some of my idols, winning competitions, and having holidays in luxurious locations with my family.

I was five under after seven holes in the British Open when the alarm went off.

------

Only two cancellations, my clients were apparently feeling intrepid today. On my drive home, my thoughts returned to Tuesday. Not last Tuesday, but next Tuesday. My adrenaline raced as I remembered my first lesson on Tuesday was with David. I have no idea why, but I was excited about delivering that lesson, and I had a feeling that it was going to be different to the others.

But I had two days and 12 more lessons to get through first.

------

On Tuesday I was up before my alarm went off. I slinked around like the pink panther getting showered and eating breakfast and out of the door without a peep from either of the children.

Unusually, there was no traffic on the roads. I arrived at the course by 6.20am. What was unusual was my motivation to get to work. This morning I was excited about my lessons. Or should I say one particular lesson, I had this feeling that today was going to be different, a good day.

I got two cups of coffee ready, added milk and stuffed some sugar in my pocket. Grabbed a handful of clubs and a basket of balls and headed out onto the driving range.

"Morning Russ!" a loud voice boomed out as I walked down the back of the bays. I spun round spilling boiling coffee down my hand.

"Argh!" I shouted, "Pete, you scared the crap out of me!"

"Sorry mate, everything ok? Good weekend?"

"Yes, most lessons showed up." I said, annoyed, "You?"

"Awesome, I took it off, spent the whole weekend watching the Dubai Classic."

I muttered an expletive under my breath as I laid the coffee and clubs down in my bay.

"You're early?" Pete observed.

"Yep, my 7 am booking. New guy. In fact, here he is now." I pointed to the car park as David's Autobiography pulled into a parking bay.

David jumped down from the Range Rover, somewhat more appropriately dressed for a game of golf. He walked towards the driving range, head high, shoulders back, but casual and relaxed.

"Morning Russ! I've been looking forward to our lesson, what's the plan?" he exclaimed as he approached.

"Up to you," I replied as he got closer, "Start where we left off?"

"More irons? You're the boss, let's go for it."

I started the lesson with a warm-up, loosening up the back, shoulders and arms before we even hit a ball. Warming up isn't just for the physical benefit of the client. Warming up means clients have less chance of injuring themselves and missing lessons. It's a good habit to get into in any sport and helps with mindset.

The lesson was going well. David was attentive and made minor adjustments as I talked him through various points of balance, posture and grip. Eventually, David struck up a conversation.

"So, how's everything been this week Russell?" David asked me inquisitively.

"Good," I said, without thinking, or knowing what to say next.

"What do you mean by good?!"

"Erm…well, I've had lessons every day, a few cancellations, so an average week." I came back. Why was he so interested in me? I thought to myself.

"What do you mean by average?" David persevered.

"Ah. 40 or so lessons booked for the week, and a few cancellations," I felt the need to add, "I've had worse!"

"And what do you mean by worse?" David kept on quizzing me.

"Well, on a bad Saturday, six out of eight clients will cancel if it rains. It did rain this Saturday, but only a couple cancelled."

"Go on." David encouraged me.

I went on to explain how I take cash on the day and how those six cancellations on that Saturday meant I'd made £50…no, £25 in fees; one of those who did turn up forgot his wallet. £5 from each booked lesson goes to the course; I'd ended up with a £15 loss on the day.

"When I was younger I wanted to be Tiger Woods and win the British Open. Touted as a rising star, I won a handful of junior competitions. But I dislocated my shoulder during a school rugby match, and my game has never been the same since."

David carried on striking golf balls as I talked. In between strokes he glanced up and nodded at me acknowledging my story. As I came to an end and paused for breath, David interrupted me, "Russ, why do you teach people how to play golf?"

"That's easy. I love the game. I know I make a difference through teaching others how to improve their game. I just want this to be my full-time job, and make a decent living out of it." I explained.

"So, let me get this right," David starting recalling my story, "Your income is based solely on delivering one-hour golf lessons at £25 per lesson. You take cash on delivery after each lesson. Most of the time they pay you and sometimes they don't. The course takes £5 of your fees regardless of whether your client turns up or not and the client doesn't pay if they don't show up. How many days a week do you work?"

"Six days, sometimes seven." I felt slightly ashamed, "David, this is your lesson by the way so don't feel that you have to talk business…"

David cut me off before I could finish, "Russell, it's ok. Call it my gift to you. I have a saying which is 'Always be the Coach' which means that if there's an opportunity to help I will always be the coach and help if that's ok with you?"

"Well, if you don't mind, then sure, but I don't want to encroach on your leisure time, and call me Russ please, only my Mother calls me Russell!"

"Don't worry Russell…sorry, Russ, I will never be a world beater at golf so it's safe to say coaching is my passion and I don't need leisure time away from it." David chuckled to himself, "Where was I, so, six sometimes seven days a week. Wow. With two kids and a wife as well. So, what's your biggest challenge at the moment?"

I thought for a few minutes. I never saw my work as a challenge before so I had to dig deep to find an answer. I thought back to what had made me angry during the past week.

"Money isn't important to me although life is a bit of a struggle because my income isn't guaranteed and regular. During the winter it drops dramatically. What gets to me is my clients not turning up. I mean, yes, if they turn up then I get paid. But..." I paused for a moment, "I just really want to teach them. I know how much of a difference golf makes to people's wellbeing, mindset, everything. I want to help people improve their game. If they don't turn up, I can't help them to better their game."

David took a moment to absorb what I had just said. He turned to address the golf ball, which happened to be the last one from the basket and gave it a purposeful thwack.

Blimey! It went dead straight, in a beautiful arc, and nestled neatly within 5 yards of the 180-yard marker. The best 3-iron David had taken in the last 59 minutes. He turned back to face me, "Russ, what if I said I could guarantee that I could get all of your clients to come to every single lesson and that you could make a little bit more money in the process?"

I was still looking stunned at the 180-yard marker and, after a second or two, returned to look at David, "You can do that? Yeah, I'd be up for that!"

"OK, here's the deal. I'm going to pay you for lessons, and if it's ok, we'll chat about your business too. All I need is for you to follow the instructions I give you each week, does that sound ok?"

"Yes!"

"The first exercise I want you to do for next Tuesday is to write up a list of your one, three, five and ten-year goals. No matter how big or small. But imagine where you want your life to be at each interval. Share your goals with your wife. Write them down for me. We'll discuss them next week." David, reached into his pocket for something, "Do you mind if I pay up front for my lessons with you?" I looked down as David handed me a bit of paper.

"Sure", I said slightly baffled.

"Great, see you next week, Russ, don't forget to write down your goals!" he said as he turned towards the car park.

When David was out of eyesight, I turned my attention to the bit of paper I had in my hands. It was a cheque. I unfolded it. The amount was for £595.00, signed David R G Marchant, dated 6th November 2016. On the back I could see a handwritten note:

"Russ, for eight lessons starting from today, thanks, David."

**28** TAKE YOUR SHOT

# CHAPTER 4: SET A GOAL

That evening I walked in through the front door to be immediately greeted by Susan, with a broad smile on her face and her finger to her lips making a, "Sshhhh!" noise. She gave me a big hug and kissed me on the cheek. It made my heart skip a beat like on our first date.

The children were asleep by 7 pm. Having the kids asleep by 7 pm was unheard of in our household. I did my best to whisper to Susan, "Darling, I've got something exciting to talk to you about, I'll cook supper, just go and relax for a bit." I put all of my positive energy into cooking a superb spaghetti Bolognese and set the table, complete with wine and candles.

When the food was ready, I ushered her into 'my restaurant' and pushed her chair under her as she sat down. I could see she had a slight frown on her face, as her gaze followed me around the kitchen. Yes, it was unusual for me to do anything remotely romantic, I knew what she was thinking. We both devoured our dinner while making the usual small talk about the children, about Ellie's day at school, and how Jacob had started rolling over and cried every time he got stuck on his front.

Eventually, Susan looked at me intently and asked, "So, Russ, what's this big news you've got for me?"

I excitedly regaled to her my tale about meeting David the week before, and the lesson we'd had earlier on today. Her eyes widened as I pulled out the cheque and showed it to her; I still didn't understand the meaning of the amount of £595 and Susan couldn't work it out either, but we both knew the money would help. I told her about how David had agreed to coach me during the next seven lessons.

"I've got such a good feeling about this, Susan; I don't know why but I feel like he can help me. Help us." I continued, "He seemed confident about the lessons and me earning more money."

"Darling, it sounds a bit fishy to me, almost too good to be true. Just be careful!"

My bubble burst momentarily, "Well, I've got nothing to lose, how I see it is that this guy has just paid me £595 to give him golf lessons while he's teaching me a bit about running a business."

"Ok!" she reiterated, "Just be careful!"

"Right, yes, be careful! Anyway, David has asked me to do an exercise with you."

"Erm…right?!"

"He wants us to talk about our goals; where do we see ourselves in the future?" I explained, "We need to write down our one, three, five and ten-year goals. He suggested I write them down and share them with you, but I'd like us to come up with them together."

Susan took a little cajoling but eventually agreed and, once we'd cleared the dirty plates from the dining room table, we decamped into the lounge. I pulled out several felt tips pens and a handful of paper, writing a heading at the top of each page. Year One. Year Three. Year Five. Year Ten.

And we started writing out our goals:

**Year One**

- Create a steady income
- Ensure clients turn up to every lesson
- …

Making a list of my goals was harder than I thought.

- Book an overseas holiday
- Buy those Jimmy Choo shoes Susan has always wanted
- Spend four hours more with the children each week
- …

Now we were getting into it.

**Year Three**

- New car
- Garden room/office
- Enough money so Susan doesn't have to work
- New kitchen
- Re-decorate the living room, and the bathroom
- No…redecorate the whole house
- Scrap that, let's just buy a new house

"Can we afford to do that Russ? I mean we're not exactly flush?" quizzed Susan.

"Susan, imagine this is a mind map which you do at work, and there are no right or wrong answers please!" I corrected her.

"But Russ this is utterly pointless if we don't have the money, surely?"

"No, Susan, this is just a bit of fun, come on you must go to bed at night dreaming about your perfect house, the children growing up, where we go on holiday?" I found myself pleading with her to go along with this.

"Russ, it's just totally unrealistic, people like us just don't live that sort of life. We're not lucky, I'm going to bed!" and with that, she left the room with me sat on the sofa feeling slightly numbed by her words. I did what every man does in this situation, and rather than comfort my wife, I carried on with the task that David had set me.

**Year Five**

- Lifetime family trip to the Gold Coast
- British Open champion
- Detached six-bedroom house on a hill with an acre of land, ponies for the children to ride, two Irish Wolfhounds by my side, a Maserati parked on the drive, I'm wearing a Rolex, Susan is walking up the steps out of our indoor pool and Derek, our gardener, is tending to the shrubs on the driveway leading down to the large wrought iron gates…

I was having great fun with the exercise by now and getting carried away,

- Mortgage free
- Kids in private school
- Bali, surfing trip
- Front cover of Golfer Magazine and 8-page interview
- Clothing, scrap that, full apparel and golf accessory range

**Year Ten**

- Retired, but working, because I love my job
- Own a golf course
- Hold regular invitational competitions

- Several of my clients are on the PGA Tour
- Played golf with Adam Sandler and Robert Wagner
- ...and Will Smith, and Matthew McConaughey
- Tesla Model X
- Private Jet
- ...

"Yes, I think that'll do nicely!" I finished my list and went to bed.

------

David listened intently with his head cocked slightly to one side as I reeled off my list of goals. When I'd finished my brain dump, he paused for a few moments, looking over my left shoulder, as he seemed to be processing my long list of demands. Finally, he turned his attention back to me. "Russ, your 'why' is clear; it's your family. Am I right?"

I nodded.

"Your purpose is golf; and what I mean by that is your talents, passion, expertise and even your core values are all based on the game of golf. It's in your DNA. Am I right?"

I nodded again.

"How you measure your life success, seems to be fairly materialistic, but this gives me a pretty good yardstick. Your 'How' is pretty obvious to me; get clients to turn up to lessons, deliver an outcome, and get paid for it."

I nodded; he seemed to know me inside and out, "Spot on, David, but how do I achieve that; get clients to every lesson and make sure they pay for their lessons?"

"We'll come onto that, Russ, but it's crucial to set out a clearly defined goal for yourself. Life without a clearly defined goal is nothing more than meaningless actions with no clear sense of direction. You have to choose a single goal to focus on and ensure that all activity is geared towards that one goal."

## David's Lesson on Setting Goals

Imagine that each of these 30 or so golf balls, which I've just rolled out on the ground, represent an activity which you do on a daily basis within your business. It could be anything from sending an email, making a telephone call, tidying the shop, getting a business card printed, sending out a mailshot, or any number of things.

The first thing you notice about the golf balls is that they look like they are laid out randomly in a bit of a mess. A mess is how most entrepreneurs treat their business on a daily basis. Jumping from one activity to the next in a random order with no real sense of direction.

How do you start to make sense of this? If I put this flag at the top of the group of balls then, all of a sudden, you have a target to aim for; or a goal. If I lay two clubs down in a 'V' shape funnelling the balls (activities) towards the goal, there are some activities which sit within the funnel. The Funnel is your customer journey leading towards the goal.

The activities furthest away from your goal are surrounded by "noise". There are lots of them, and ultimately you will have no idea if doing these activities will help you to achieve your goal. Every time you're about to start an activity in your business ask yourself this question, "Will this activity take me closer to my goal?"

If the answer is no - David knocks away a few balls on the periphery - as an entrepreneur, your gut instinct is pretty powerful, and 90% of the time you will be right. 10% of the time you will be wrong. The quickest way to fail is through procrastination. If you make the decision quickly and you get it wrong, you can pivot and pull yourself back on track.

The BIGGEST mistake entrepreneurs make is chasing the next new shiny thing. What starts out as an activity which gets you closer to your goal quickly turns into an idea and starts a chain of events which results in a new goal; taking you away from your initial goal that you set for yourself. About two activities into "new shiny thing" you realise that this is now a distraction but for several reasons; fear of failure, fear of letting people down, and fear of not finishing what you started you carry on regardless.

I spent ages organising an event the previous year aimed at attracting new players. All I succeeded in doing was annoying existing members by not inviting them and offering discounted fees to new players. Four people turned up to the event.

Now that you know this, you can pivot quickly and bring yourself back on track with your goal. All it takes is discipline and remembering your 'why'. Once you have cut through the noise and you start to move closer to your goal, both you and your customers start to gain clarity around a) what your goal is b) how achievable it is and c) the activities required to achieve it which now number just a few.

Finally, your message hits home, and you start to chip away at your goal bit by bit.

My model is based on the principles of Think and Grow Rich by an author named Napoleon Hill. It is a fantastic book, but the "secret" Hill mentions is based on goals. Firstly, you have to have a specific goal. Secondly, you have to have a strong desire to achieve that goal. Finally, you must take positive action to achieve that goal.

Think of the people who base their future prosperity on winning the lottery. I read a study recently where 60 percent of people do just that, base their future wealth on winning the lottery. They were then asked, "Do you buy lottery tickets?" to which 48% replied yes. That means 52% of the 60% of people questioned had a desire to win the lottery but didn't buy a ticket. Along with a similar analogy, luck can be created. Who creates more luck; the person who buys one ticket or the person who buys ten?

A goal must be explicit and measured over a given length of time.

Let's take your business, Russ. If you wanted to earn £100,000 in the next 12 months that would be a very specific goal that is measured over a set length of time. You MUST break it down further. That £100k is made up by your clients paying you. If each client pays you £500 over the course of a year, you would need to attract 200 clients into your program. Or if your program generated £2,000 per client, you only need 50 clients per year.

I'm sure that if you achieved an income of £100k in the next 12 months, you can have that overseas holiday, buy Susan the Jimmy Choos, and have some extra time with your kids. Heck! The new car, new house and even Susan giving up work will become a reality.

------

"You idiot!" I kept telling myself. I didn't believe a local golf professional, like myself, could earn £100k per year.  It wasn't my clients who were the problem; it was me. All this time I had been playing too small. I had never given a thought to how much I wanted to earn each year.

My mind was racing, "OK, David, how? How do I do it? What have I got to do to do exactly that, the car, the shoes, the holiday, clients at EVERY lesson? Getting paid? How?"

# CHAPTER 5: CREATE A PRODUCT

That night I went to bed imagining what it would be like to be making a serious living from golf lessons. I had no idea what had happened during the 60 minutes I spent with David that Tuesday morning but, for the first time since launching my business, I felt a burning and overwhelming desire to succeed.

All I kept thinking about was my desire to achieve my goals. Not just the one-year goals but now my three and five-year goals seemed possible. Not only that, but they seemed achievable within 12 months. "I can do this!" was all that kept running through my mind, "I can do this!"

I barely slept for the next two nights. I was, however, brought right back down to earth with a bump on Thursday. 2 cancellations rang in by 7 am but, honestly, I was starting not to care about these anymore. I took it as given that it was a part of the job, people were unreliable. I was using my new found future prosperity as an excuse to ignore the no-shows.

It was a double whammy when I got called into Richard's office as soon as I arrived. Richard was the owner of the course, in his early 60's, fairly svelte but balding, and always smartly dressed. Richard tended not to want to speak to me unless something had gone wrong.

Pete had already taken his seat in Richard's office.

The second-hand golf clubs. I knew immediately. I sat down in the chair next to Pete.

"So chaps," Richard started, "The cash register was down in the shop last week, I guess it's the same issue with the second-hand equipment?" I shot Pete a glare, expecting him to speak first. Pete said nothing. Richard looked at me, "There are about 25 clubs with no purchase price against them on the list." Pete still said nothing, "I'd say we are about £590 down, and I expect you both to cover the cost." Pete still said nothing. I got up to leave, "Fine." I exhaled walking towards the door.

As Pete followed me out I waited until we were out of earshot of Richard's office, "Pete, why didn't you say anything?" he stared at me, "You lost the bloody sheet last week. Why didn't you tell me? I need the money, you idiot!"

------

I discovered why Pete said nothing; he didn't show up for work on Friday…or Saturday, and by Monday I knew he wasn't coming back, he'd quit and wanted to ensure he stood a chance of getting a good reference. The good news for me was that I made back the shortfall in equipment sales by taking Pete's lessons over the coming weeks.

------

Tuesday couldn't have come around sooner. David listened as I regaled what had happened during the previous week. Finally, he chipped in, "How do you feel about Pete right now, Russ? You need to move on. Despite the fact you benefited financially from Pete's ineptitude, you are still holding onto something. Time to let it go and move on." I nodded. "Do you want me to tell you what business coaching is?" I nodded again, "I'm a bit like a personal trainer, I show you all of the exercises and educate you on your nutrition. However, I am not going to put your trainers on and go running for you. Plus you have to be in the right frame of mind, the right mode, to be receptive of coaching otherwise none of it will stick. So, are you ready to move on?"

"Definitely!" I said as assertively as I could, feeling stunned at how David had snapped me out of my funk.

"Today I want to talk about your product. It was something you didn't say when we first met which surprised me. It struck me as a quick win that we can get for you right away."

**David's Lesson on Creating Products**

When we first met, you made an immediate first impression on me, Russ, but for the wrong reasons, pleasantly though as you are a friendly chap. You made up for not sticking to the rules by exuding a warm and friendly charisma, which you have in bucket loads by the way.

My issue wasn't with the "how", you are an excellent tutor; I am more concerned about your onboarding process. As a new client, you allowed me to lead the sale and the first lesson. It is the initial conversation and transaction which sets the stage for the rest of the performance.

What I mean by that is you asked me a handful of vague questions about my golf game, and never explained to me what your lessons involved or what the result – the value proposition – would be once I had completed your course. Your sales pitch wasn't even about delivering a course of lessons; it was more about when can we get started?

Your enthusiasm, unfortunately, can be mistaken for a sign of desperation and reduces your credibility. So, today, we are going to fix that.

You must remember that you are NOT selling golf lessons. You are selling a result – this is your product. You cannot sell one product either; you must offer an element of choice. To do this, and provide guaranteed results, you must niche your products and focus on one specific area of your client's game.

The most important lesson is that most people have some form of intelligence, right? When it comes to your products and services, they have absolutely none. Which means that you must lead your clients, and NOT be led by them otherwise they will have a very unauthentic experience which will fizzle out very quickly. You will spend most of your time onboarding new clients, deliver a handful of lessons, they will stop showing up and eventually not come back at all.

Your product must have a set of features which provide a guaranteed result for your clients. It must be delivered over a set period of time. It must be recognisable – this is called *packaging*.

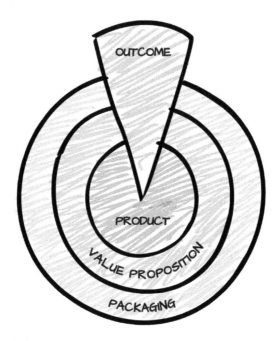

I thought for a minute about my clients not turning up and then ebbing away. I had no idea why, until now. It was starting to make sense, "You're right, David, that is exactly what's happening. I'm not sure about how to create products out of lessons, isn't it a service I offer?"

"Yes, it is a service, but how you package your service and price it is what turns it into a product. Have you noticed that I have only been using the 3-iron at every lesson so far?" asked David. I had, and I thought it was a bit odd. "This was on purpose, the worst part of my game is my long irons. I figured if I spent eight lessons using the 3-iron, my long iron game would improve." It already had. David was already hitting it straighter and about 30 yards further after three lessons.

"What other areas of the game do people most often ask you to help them improve on, Russ?" David had stopped and turned face-on to me now, looking at me intently.

"Driving further, driving more accurately, lowering putting average and handicap and then chipping around the green," I replied.

 The penny dropped. The services I offered were indeed products; I just hadn't packaged them up. Even the service I thought I was offering wasn't a service as I was just selling hours of my time.

"There you go, Russ, those are your five signature products. When a new prospect comes into your shop, ask them the right questions and offer them one of those five products. In fact, don't offer it, advise them on which product they need."

"Are you saying I just do endless lessons covering one area of their game until they become good at it?" This concept made me feel uncomfortable. The club used more than any other club is the putter which is used for 40% of the shots per round. I spend a proportional amount of time practising with each club to improve ALL aspects of my client's game.

"I am, and I know what you're thinking, the putter is the most used club, and you need to spend a proportional amount of time across all clubs to improve their overall game. Russ, if you improve one area of their game you make their ENTIRE game better. And don't forget, you are their trainer, you can furnish them with a plan. Give them the tips but allow them to spend 40% of their time practising with the putter. You don't need to do that DURING the lessons." David continued, "Let's drill down on that word, endless, which you used. The short answer is no! How many lessons would it take for you to help someone drive 30 yards further off the tee?"

"8 weeks, maybe, if they show up to every lesson."

"OK, what else? How could you turn that maybe into a definite?"

"Well, they need to practice outside of lessons, it's all creating muscle memory as that fades after three days or so."

"Brill, how many times in between lessons?" David kept pushing me.

"Two, maybe three, three if they wanted to achieve longer distances off the tee." The penny dropped again, "Got you, I need to deliver a specific result, over a defined length of time, and the only way to guarantee that is to focus on one aspect of the game?"

"You got it, Russ, now, how do you know if they've practised between lessons? Could you ask your clients to send you a photo of themselves practising between lessons, a selfie on the driving range perhaps?" David smiled, pulling a ridiculous pose like he was taking a selfie.

"Absolutely!" I said, "But how do I know they're not creating a bank of photos and just sending them through without actually going to the driving range?"

"Modern technology, Russ, it's called GPS and a timestamp!"

For the first time since starting the business, I felt a sense of certainty. An incredibly specific offering for my clients, and an answer as to why they weren't attending lessons. It was evident, why hadn't I seen this before? But, hey! I was just grateful I had seen the light now, what a great opportunity.

David and I said our goodbyes, and I watched David gather up his coat and head back towards his Range Rover. I looked at his car again, "I'm going to have one of those one day," I thought to myself.

I couldn't wait to test out my new products, and I didn't have to wait long. At lunch time, two chaps walked into the shop inquiring about lessons. I took the opportunity, "Gentlemen, how can I help you?" they indicated that they were interested in lessons, "What area of your game are you most looking to improve on?"

"My driving is terrible; I've got a draw on my driver which I can't seem to put right." Said the first. The other chap followed up with, "Actually, similar, although he always seems to out-drive me… when he manages to hit the fairway!" They both laughed.

Seizing the opportunity, I said, "I've got the perfect program for you. An 8-week course which, by the end of it, you will be driving straighter, and you will be driving further. How does that sound?"

"Perfect," they said in near perfect unison, "Where do we sign?
I booked them both into the diary with a joint lesson offering a
slight discount at £20 per lesson each for eight weeks.

I felt elated, at the top of my game.

# CHAPTER 6: TAKE YOUR SHOT

I couldn't wait to tell David the news, so I sent David a text message;

*"Hi David, hope you don't mind me messaging you, but I just sold two chaps onto an 8-week course. How about that, thank you!!! KR, Russ."*

I didn't hear anything back from David for about 2 hours;

"Wow Russ, congratulations, you are now selling 'products' and not services. Did you get to the bottom of 'why' they want to have lessons with you?"

I thought for a moment, "No, damn, I remember David saying this was important, but why?" I tried to recall; I typed out another message;

*"I remember you mentioned something but, I'm not sure I remember exactly, any tips?"*

"Sure Russ, you've got to find out two 'whys' 1) why do your clients want to improve their golf game? And 2) why they chose you? – good luck, flying to NY, about to board!"

Now, this was a bit of a mystery to me. I had never thought to ask my clients, so I didn't know the answer to either question. I had several days before I saw David again to find out.

In the meantime, my brother had been in touch to see if I was free at the weekend to make up a foursome with him and a couple of his work buddies. Somehow I'd managed to settle my diary down somewhat so I could take Saturday off, and Susan was taking the kids to stay with their grandparents for the weekend. I could get out and play some golf for a change rather than just hit a few balls in between lessons with clients.

My brother and I had started playing golf at about the same time. Being three years older than me, he was a much better golfer until we reached our teens. For some reason when I reached 13 I started to out-drive him. He began to turn his attention to girls and football rather than playing golf with his annoying little brother. He finally picked up the clubs again after University but never quite got back to where he was as a 16-year-old.

------

The round started in the usual manner, with the four of us gathered on the first tee, and my brother encouraging the four of us into a small bet. Whoever had the highest round would pick up the tab afterwards. Perfect for me as I never had to buy a round. I was still thinking about David's question, when my brother, Stu, chimed in, "Come on Russ, are you playing?" We spoofed to see who would be teeing off first which, uncharacteristically, I won the honour.

I pondered my club selection; a driver to carry the two bunkers either side of the fairway or a five wood to lay up slightly before them but leave myself a five iron to the green? I reached for the driver. Went through a couple of practice swings, checked for any wind and walked to the tee. Stu dutifully encouraged me, "Come on Russ, take your shot buddy! Don't make us wait all day!" A running joke between us; Stu always interrupted my routine on the first tee, which he found hilarious, but I wasn't listening.

I swung the driver. It made a beautiful "thwack" as it contacted the ball. It felt good. I caught sight of the ball at the top of its arc; so straight; it sailed beyond the bunkers…by miles!

"Wow! Awesome shot Russ! That's...wow!" said a somewhat astounded Keith, Stu's work colleague, "That's gotta be 300 yards?" As Stu passed me on the way to the tee, he offered me a fist bump, "Great drive bro!"

------

Stu and Keith wandered off down the fairway; their other colleague Simon leant towards me, "So, Stu tells me you're a golf pro?" I nodded. "That drive was awesome, we've got a charity tournament coming up in a couple of months, and well, you just saw my drive, the Managing Director of the company will be there, and I don't want to look like a prat. If I could hit the ball even half as good as you, I think I'd be happy." I explained my 8-week package and whether it was distance or accuracy he wanted, although I knew it was accuracy given we were in the rough hunting for Simon's ball. When I got to the package costs, he seemed a little bit surprised, "Really? How much?"

"Is that too expensive?" I immediately blurted out.

"No, Russ! Too cheap buddy, far too cheap." He retorted, "If you can make me drive like you in eight weeks, I'd give up my left nut!"

------

Somewhere between holes four and five, it clicked. I found myself grinning from ear to ear. I had worked out the answers to David's questions. The answer was obvious. That little fist-bump my brother gave me; the silent acknowledgement when given by one's superior; Stuart wanting to impress his boss; two simple words which Keith uttered, "Awesome shot!". The recognition of being at the best of one's game. That's why people want to play golf.

If you practice and become good at something, it becomes more enjoyable. The satisfaction of how the perfect shot feels, and feeling in total control of your swing so you can create that feeling time and time again.

I shot across to Simon again, and waited for him to dig his ball out of the bunker before approaching him, "Why me Simon? There are tonnes of great golf pros out there, but why would you choose me over them?"

"It's obvious, Russ, you're Stu's brother, and he does nothing but talk about how amazing a golfer you are. Plus your approach is brilliant, a simple program of eight lessons. I love the fact there's a guaranteed outcome at the end of eight weeks. It's a no-brainer for me."

Confidence is something I'd always struggled overcoming. I'd never reached the top of my game or entered any prestigious tournaments. Choosing always to sign up for the ones I had a good shot at winning. Being called 'the best' makes me feel uncomfortable. I was always proud whenever a client got good results and improved their game. I never felt like I was good despite others telling me I was.

What was it Stu said on the first tee?

 Take your shot. TAKE YOUR SHOT!

He was right; I'd helped others out for so long but never taken my shot. Taking my shot isn't about me at all. Taking my shot is about helping my clients, and I've taken the easy way out of everything. I'm not the best, but I was never trying to be the best.

If I pushed to be the best, then I can bring my clients up and on the journey with me. The objective isn't about golf at all; it's about inspiring others to be the best. Show them what they can achieve.

TAKE YOUR SHOT!

I texted David, "Got it!! 1) Because they want to enjoy the game more and get recognition for it and 2) because I can inspire them to strive to be the best golfer they can be – those are my 'whys'!!!"

I waited for what seemed like an eternity for a reply.

"You got it, Russ, that's why you're doing it! Looking forward to seeing you on Tuesday."

# CHAPTER 7: MAKE MORE MONEY

Keith, Stu and Simon funnelled into the bar, exhilarated from their round of golf. There was lots of joshing of Simon. With a terrible card of 96, our lunch and beers were definitely on Simon today. The only time I'd paid for a round was when I had forgotten my clubs, and the only set Stu could find, apparently, was a left-handed set. Even then I was only a single stroke behind Stu after the 18th.

As Simon was ordering the drinks at the bar, Richard walked in with some of his cronies. I thought I'd seen his car in the car park. He instantly made a bee-line for me; placing his hand on my shoulder, he proudly introduced me to the rest of his foursome, "Guys, I want to introduce you, this is one of my lackeys, Russell. He's a busy guy at the moment as Pete, the other pro, buggered off and left us all in a jam!" He laughed; I shot him a look, and his buddies all swarmed in to shake my hand. "Who's buying, Russell? Ah! Is that your elusive brother? Alright, Stu?"

Stu just nodded and continued to help Simon carry the drinks over to our table.

Then Richard, without even any hint of discretion, fired a shot at me, "Russell, when you're next in can you swing by the office, I want to talk to you about your fees." His statement meant only one thing; he was putting them up, again, for the second time this year.

When we'd all sat down, Stu leant across to me, "What a fool! I can't believe you're still working for that idiot. Have you looked into any other courses yet?" I had briefly had a look around and had spotted a driving range on my commute which would work,

"Yeah, there's a driving range on the outskirts of Thame which would be perfect. I'm just working out how I can take all of my clients with me without upsetting them too much." Stu raised his glass, "Sounds like a good move, little bro', life's too short to be working with muppets like that, cheers."

Simon and Keith joined in, and we all raised our glasses in unison, "To the Muppets!"

------

I returned home just after 6.30pm, and to my surprise, the house was surprisingly quiet as I walked in through the door. Susan, greeted me as I pushed the front door open.

"Wowsers, darling!" I was stunned, "You look beautiful!" Susan was wearing a lovely blue, lace dress, full face of makeup, hair straightened, legs out, and she looked stunning, "Are you going out?" Susan put her finger to her lips, "Shhhh, darling! The children are in bed and asleep, your mother's popping over in about ten minutes to babysit for us. I'm not going out; we're going out."

I couldn't remember the last time we'd been out. Not least because we couldn't afford it, but frequently both Susan and I were exhausted and in bed by 9 pm. I shot up the stairs like a whippet and popped on the shirt Susan had laid out on the bed for me, already ironed. I squirted some Hugo Boss and fluffed my hair around a bit so that I looked at least semi-presentable. My mother was already here by the time I went downstairs, I gave her a quick kiss, and she watched us out of the door with her customary, "Have fun kids!"

"Where are we going?" I asked as Susan led me out the door. "Just to the local Italian, darling, I thought it would be fun. How was your round today?"...

------

The weekend seemed a far cry away, and it was Tuesday before I knew it. Eagerly waiting for David to arrive so that we could get to work on my next lesson. I couldn't believe how quickly six weeks had gone by already and how much had changed in such a small amount of time. I said as much to David when he arrived.

"Time flies, hey, Russ? It's something I come across all the time with my clients. I have a saying which is – one overestimates how much you can achieve in a month, but underestimate how much one can accomplish in a year. Just imagine where you could be in 12 months, Russ." David was right; I couldn't believe how far I'd already come, "David, why is that? Why have I been able to do so much in such a short period?"

"Simple, Russ, you've just focused on one thing. Creating better systems and processes for your business. You were too busy concentrating on too many little things, fire-fighting one might say. And, I hope you don't mind me saying, you were focussing too much on you and not on your clients. Now that you're focussing more on what your clients want, your business is free to prosper."

As always, David was right. As I tipped the bucket of balls out ready for David to get started, I asked him, "What's the plan for today then?"

David scooped a ball towards his feet with the head of the club and positioned it on the mat, "What's your biggest challenge now we've created some products, and you've been able to sign some clients up?"

I took a moment to think about this as David took a few practice swings.

"How do I make more money?"

David looked up, "My favourite topic, Russ!"

**David's Lesson on the 3 Common Pricing Mistakes**

The first common pricing mistake is charging an hourly rate for services. A business might be charging £25 per hour, for example. Why is this a mistake? As the owner of a startup business, you will likely have done little if any, market or competitor research. You charge what you feel is right and by the value, you place on yourself.

Time and again I see business owners undervaluing themselves; you can always be charging more for your products and services.

If you are charging time for money, you can never get that time back. Once you've sold yourself for an hour, for £25, you can never get that hour back. You've got to maximise your earning potential for every hour that you work. You can always make more money, but you can never make any more time, therefore, selling an hour of your time is like selling your soul.

If you're charging at an hourly rate, double-check how much you're charging. Also, check what capacity you have. If you are always busy working and delivering a service 40 hours per week then now might be the time to consider putting your hourly rate up or introducing a day-rate for new projects.

The second mistake is to charge what everybody else is charging.

How do you know whether what everybody else is charging, is the right amount? And the answer to that is, you don't. While all of your competitors might be charging the same price; they might all be wrong. You have to charge based on the value of the outcome you can deliver for your clients, and incrementally add more value to provide a better quality service and charge more.

You can test the marketplace by putting a price out there to gauge whether there is resistance. Here is a scenario and I want you to ask yourself whether you have made this mistake:

Ten people might buy your product, and most are happy with the outcome. But there's this one prospect who comes back to you and says, "Gosh, David, that's expensive."

Who do we tend to listen to? That's right, the one person who says your products and services are expensive, not the ten individuals who bought at the price you set. Do not react to the one person who provides negative feedback. Listen to the positive feedback you are getting and how many products and services you are already selling.

That leads me to the third common mistake around pricing – not being brave enough whenever you look to increase your prices.

Whenever I challenge my clients to put their prices up, they immediately have a mental picture in their mind of all their existing clients leaving in droves.

Your clients are getting a product or service at a particular price, so if you put your prices up, well, yes, some clients are going to be unhappy and likely leave. To reassure existing clients you can gradually increment your prices or add more value, so it is less painful for them.

Rest assured, if your clients are raving fans, they will not leave you and will support your business through any price rises. Most importantly, new prospects won't yet have been exposed to your prices, so you can charge them whatever you like, within reason.

By putting your products into packages, Russ, you can now overcome all three mistakes by charging what you like for your eight-week program.

------

The next question was obvious, "So, how much do you propose I charge for my eight-week course, David?"

David leant on his club and looked me straight in the eye, "Take a guess, Russ!"

I racked my brains; as usual, David already knew the answer, and normally it's obvious. I had a flash if inspiration, "The cheque you gave me; £595. You think I can charge £595 for eight  lessons of golf? That's insane. No-one charges that much around here for lessons. Ah! The three pricing mistakes, £25 an hour. How do I know the competition are right?"

"Yes," David agreed, "And be brave!"

# CHAPTER 8: SIGN ON THE DOTTED LINE

"What on earth are you doing, Russ?" Susan looked at me quizzically. I don't blame her; it was 5 am on Saturday morning. Still, pitch black outside, and I was pulling on my cycling gear for the first time in at least two years.

"Just going out for a quick ride, darling. My two new guys aren't due at the course until 10 am so I wanted to get a few miles in before heading into work."

Bearing in mind, it was now the middle of December and only about 4 degrees outside. I took a sharp intake of breath as I stepped out the door and had a very brief moment of, "What the heck are you doing, Russ?!" before heading out to the garage to get my bike and helmet.

When Elena was born, I used to do the 4 am feed and jump straight on my bike afterwards as she would usually sleep through until about 7 am. The freedom we once had seemed to dissipate after Jacob was born. They would tag-team match against Susan and me to see how long they could keep us awake at night. I used to love my early morning rides, and now with my new found freedom at work, I'd got a little bit more time back. My confidence was growing to do more of the things I used to do without fearing the impact it would have on Susan and the children as well.

As I rode off out into the darkness, freshly charged lights blazing, I discovered an all too familiar feeling. Like those projects and adventures, I used to have as a child. I got straight out of the saddle and motored out of town and into the countryside.

------

Two hours and 35 miles later I returned home slightly weary. Hands blackened from the double puncture I'd had to change. The experience of changing the tubes was an interesting one though. A car had gone to overtake me but saw I was struggling in the dark. He then reversed up behind me and popped his lights onto the full beam. I regaled the story to Susan over breakfast, and I could sense that my enthusiasm was infecting her, "Can I go for a run when you get back this afternoon, Russ? That would be fun."

------

"What on earth have you been doing?" David asked me as I hobbled over to collect his basket of balls.

"Cycling, David, possibly a bit too far as it's been a while since I last went out on the bike. I only did 35 miles and could barely walk yesterday let alone teach a lesson." I was so stiff after my ride, but it had made me realise that I needed to make a long-term commitment to my fitness. Being physically fit makes the golf game so much easier. "I need to do more exercise. I'd always thought I'd get it out onto the course, but mostly I'm just stood giving lessons and not doing anything myself."

David chuckled at me, "Russ! You should know by now that you need to get your time a little bit more organised. Could you cycle to the course, or leave a little earlier to go for a run? Better still, when you make a bit more money do one fewer lesson a day and spend some time on your own game and fitness."

"You make it sound so incredibly simple, David, I'm still not sure about charging £595 for eight lessons, it feels too much. I don't know who's going to pay that much." I responded negatively.

"Russ, Russ, Russ! There's only one way to find out."

## David's Lesson on Pitching Products and Getting Commitment

You may have heard the saying that, "Done is better than perfect." Well, this is a simplified version of the lessons taught by Eric Reis in his book, The Lean Startup. Too many entrepreneurs and business owners spend weeks, months or even years perfecting their product before taking it to market. By which point they've neglected to create a customer base for their products and when they launch no-one wants it.

Reis suggests creating shorter feedback loops throughout product development and inviting 'early adopters' to come on board during that process to provide real-time feedback on any problems they're having or features which are missing.

Imagine spending 12 months perfecting your golf program only to find out that no-one wants it, for any number of different reasons. However, if you pitch a basic version of your golf program and launch it within a month, you can test the marketplace immediately. Every month you improve the course, a bit like what Steve Brailsford did with the Sky Cycling team in preparation for the 2012 Olympics. He introduced a system of 'marginal gains'; if we shave a gramme off here, it will save us a second there.

We live in a remarkable age now where we have an opportunity to pitch a mere idea without having any product or prototype built. You can buy a ticket to a local networking event, and pitch your idea to the first person you meet. Pitching an idea is primary 'market research'. Imagine the first person doesn't like the idea, so you tweak your pitch, and the second person gets it. Maybe they more than get it, maybe they ask you, "Can we meet for a coffee? I'd love to hear more about that."

At this point I could hear Richard's voice in the distance, "Russ! Russ!" I turned around, "Can I have a word with you?"

"Richard, can this wait please, I'm with a client," I said sharply.

"No! I've just heard you did a group lesson on Saturday and that's not what we agreed. Not only that but you're supposed to be signing new clients up to membership meetings with me. I checked their names at reception, and I've seen neither book on. In fact, none of your clients has been to see me in the last month. So, what the hell is going on?"

"Richard, please, I'm with a client." I ushered Richard away out of earshot of David.

"So, come on? What's going on?"

"Richard, our agreement was that I would pay you a fee per hour for every lesson booked and that I would offer them a membership brochure to take away. The double lesson was two friends who wanted a joint lesson. What's the problem?"

"Do I have to do everything myself, just sell some damned memberships, or you're out of here alright." Richard just turned and walked off. I walked back round to see David hammer a 3-iron straight down the centre of the driving range. "Awesome, David, no tips from me, that was perfect!"

"I've a good teacher, Russ. Who was that?"

"Nobody, well Richard, the owner of the course. He likes to get on my case now and then. I think it's an ego thing."

"Maybe I should have a word with him," David winked at me, "Now where was I?"

So, you now have a suite of products to offer prospects; you have a guaranteed outcome for them over the course of eight weeks, provided they do the work and, finally, you have a fixed price for delivering the agreed outcome. Now all you need is a way of getting a commitment from your prospects up front. Something that they will feel obligated to commit 100% to and know that if they don't do what they've agreed with you, they will not achieve the desired outcome.

You have a product here which you can now pitch, but it needs formalising somehow into a brochure or contract.

David pulls out a notepad from his bag at this point, opens it to a blank page and starts sketching something out.

When someone completes a sign-up form like this one, they are not only making a commitment to you, but also to themselves. A commitment which states that if they don't do everything agreed in the contract you won't be able to offer them a 100% money back guarantee.

Many business owners baulk at this. The main reason for them baulking is that they lack clarity and confidence in their products and services. Therefore if they lack confidence in their products, how are they supposed to be able to demonstrate that confidence to their prospects?

By writing your 'pitch' down in black and white ink on some paper, it makes a service tangible. And that is how to productize a service, raise your prices and build confidence in your offering. Get the prospect to make a commitment to you and not vice-versa because that commitment is already taken care of by the service you offer.

Wow, it almost seemed too simple. I don't know why I never 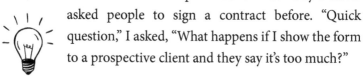 asked people to sign a contract before. "Quick question," I asked, "What happens if I show the form to a prospective client and they say it's too much?"

"Simple, Russ, you don't have to print out hundreds of sign-up forms. I must also emphasise at this point that I might not be right, but you've got to pitch something to gain the feedback I mentioned earlier on. I propose you print out ten copies, maybe, and try it out on the first ten people who come into the shop asking for lessons." David carried on, "That was if all ten say it's far too expensive, you can adjust the price. But, what I do want you to do, is put this offer to ten people and see how it goes."

I paused for a moment to peruse David's sketched form, "You mentioned a 100% money back guarantee?"

"Yes, you're an excellent tutor, a 100% money back guarantee is a great way of demonstrating confidence in your products without it sounding like a gimmick. I would introduce a simple self-assessment process too at this stage. You want your clients to decide whether they've improved their game or not over eight weeks. I would have a simple ten point assessment which you get them to complete at the start and end of the course. If they quibble the result, you can always show them their completed self-assessment form which I can guarantee will show improved results."

"Great, I'm in. I'll get ten printed up and give it a shot, David. This is gold-dust. Thank you!"

"I'm just doing my job, Russ." David offered his notepad to me while I took a photo of the sign-up form.

# RHA GOLF

## ① Outcome

- ☐ Drive 30 yards further
- ☐ Chipping around the green
- ☐ Hit the fairway
- ☐ Lower putting average
- ☐ Lower handicap by 10

---

## ② I agree to:

- ☐ Turn up all 8 lessons
- ☐ Practice 3x per week between lessons

---

## ③ Cost - £595 - Paid in full upfront for the 8 week programme

---

## ④ Sign and Date:

Name: _____

Signature: _____  Date: _____

**66** TAKE YOUR SHOT

# CHAPTER 9: WOW!

I pushed Ctrl+P, and the printer jumped into life.

Ten copies of my new product brochure streamed out of the old printer that sat underneath the sales desk. The black ink looked like it was running out, but done is better than perfect. I popped the freshly printed brochures into a folder and slid them underneath the counter. I was careful not to mark the envelope with anything; if Richard found the new forms, he'd be sure to pester me until I told him what they were for and when he discovered how much I was charging he'd also likely ask for more money.

There's so much I'd do with the golf course if Richard wasn't around, or if I owned it even better. Maybe that should be one of my goals later on; to buy the course from Richard and do all of the things I want to do with it.

My daydream was punctuated by the ringing of the shop doorbell as someone walked in. It had been raining persistently throughout the night and this morning so I'd had a couple of cancellations. One of those things I would change on the course would be to add a second level of bays in the driving range and cover them over – at least then there would be no excuses for people cancelling lessons.

The chap wandered straight over to me, "Hi there, I'm looking for Russ."

"That's me!" I said.

"Awesome. I'd like some lessons. I was at drinks last week with Simon, and he recommended I pop in and see you. He said you're the best pro in the area."

"Great, what's your name?" I asked.

"It's Ed, nice to meet you." We shook hands.

"Great to meet you, Ed. What specifically are you looking to achieve through having lessons?" I started my sales pitch. The pitch felt new. It felt different. It felt exciting. I found myself asking some specific questions and guided Ed through the five products. "So, you want to lower your handicap? How would you feel if I said I could achieve that in eight weeks using my signature 'Lower Your Handicap by 10' package?" I fell silent after asking this question as David has instructed me.

"I'm interested, how much does it cost?" Ed responded, and I could feel my stomach knotting up.

"£595 for the eight-week program, which may seem expensive for lessons however I offer a 100% money back guarantee. If you're not happy at the end of the course or don't feel we've achieved your objective, I will refund all of the money." I went silent again while reaching for the brochures under the desk, trying to maintain eye contact with Ed.

Ed pondered the offer for a moment, "What's the catch?"

"No catch. It's simple really, all I ask of you is to make a commitment to the program for the full eight weeks." I popped a brochure down on the desk facing towards Ed, "You have to agree to show up for all eight lessons, and also practice at least two times in between lessons. Otherwise, you lose the guarantee." Again, I waited silently for a response.

For what seemed like an eternity, Ed wrestled with the maths in his brain. Eventually, he picked up a pen from off the desk and signed the bottom of the sheet. It was that easy. No, surely it can't be that easy? It is though; he just signed it. Payment. PAYMENT!

"How do I pay you, Russ?" asked Ed.

I pulled out my credit card terminal and connected it to my phone, took Ed's card, popped it into the card reader, and punched in 5-9-5-0-0. Ed entered in his pin number. The card reader's status icon turned green. There it is; £595, winging across to my bank.

"Thank you, Ed, here's your card. Let's get your first lesson booked in."

------

 By the close of play on Saturday I had signed up two more clients under the new package. Not only that but they had signed a commitment saying they would be there for every lesson. And the first card payment had already hit my bank account. It felt a bit like a game. And I was winning.

The three sign-ups accounted for more money in one week than I'd made in the entire previous month before that. I texted David, "You are a wizard, David, I've signed up three new clients this week alone. Plus two have taken forms away to think about it."

"Congratulations, Russ! It's a pleasure. You get what you ask for after all. And you asked for £595 for delivering an eight-week course."

And then another message pinged through.

"By the way, I want you to think about why this is working for you. Here's a video I want you to watch before next Tuesday."

The message contained a link to a video on David's website. The video appeared to be of David sitting in a study, with wooden clad walls, and with him sat behind a broad wooden desk facing the camera.

**David's Lesson on Customer Journeys**

Most people have some form of intelligence, we hope! But when it comes to your products and services they have absolutely none. Prospects may think they know what you do. However, I can guarantee they have no idea about what your products do, how you work, or how your systems and processes work. They have no idea how you deliver your goods and/or how much time you take to deliver your goods and services relates to the cost of them. Most of all they have no idea whether your product or service is right for them or what the outcome of using your product or service will produce for them.

To overcome this, you have to create something called a 'customer journey'. During the client's journey, you are holding your prospect by the hand and leading them through your entire process, from initial meeting to delivering your products and into the aftercare and support. If you let go of their hand at any point during this process, you will more than likely lose your prospect.

You only have to remember three words in sales; know, like and trust.

Prospects can get to know you through videos, your website, networking events and social media but they can't get to like you or trust you until you sit down with them on a one-to-one basis. In the age of the internet we seem to want to skip coffee and move prospects straight into a sale, but this is no way to build long-lasting, trusted relationships with your clients.

The aim of the game, when someone first knows of you, is to move your prospect into coffee. During the initial coffee meeting, asking the right questions is vital.

I was coaching a client last week and overheard a conversation between a sales executive and the hotel manager. During the first fifteen minutes of their conversation, the sales rep didn't once ask any questions about the hotel, the hotel manager or their objectives. Their meeting ended with a, "No! Not now, thank you." I wonder, had the sales exec asked more questions, whether the hotel manager would have liked and trusted the sales exec more?

Remember, your prospects have absolutely no idea about your systems, processes, or outcomes to be had from your products and services. Which is why a commitment is imperative. The contract means that your prospect is committing to your system or process. Even if they don't fully understand it, their brain is telling them to, "Trust the process."

The customer journey doesn't end when the sale is complete; there are still two more steps to complete. The first is delivering your product to the same standard you promised during your sales pitch and in your contract. Finally, once the product is delivered, you absolutely MUST have a follow-up process to ensure your client is happy for a period after you've delivered the product to them. They might be experiencing buyer's remorse and nipping this in the bud before they leave a negative review could save your reputation.

You will start to realise that business is just a game. I say a game because games are fun and business is fun when you make it fun. Games have rules that every player must abide by. Your success is defined when your work is your passion; you create the rule book for your business. It's not defined by how much work you do to make the business function.

My challenge to those watching this video is to go away now and map out your perfect customer journey. Draw it like a flow diagram, so you can see each of the steps your customers take along the way. See the relationship build between each step.

When you receive a poor review, or a client is unhappy with the service you offered, take a look back over your customer journey. Did you lead them through every step on the customer journey?

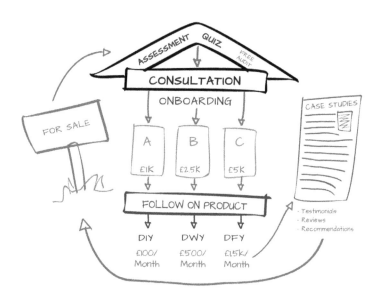

I realised now that there was so much of the customer journey that I had forgotten. One of Stu's friends had mentioned how reviews in business were incredibly powerful, and I'd never fully understood why, but now I got it; social-proof. I'd neglected some of the poor reviews, mostly down to my ego, but hadn't thought about the negative impact they might be having on my business.

Well now was the time to put that straight; I set about drawing out my customer journey as per David's instructions. It then became apparent that those clients who had either drifted away or left negative reviews hadn't completed every step in my customer journey.

It was obvious. Systemising my golf lessons has turned it into a product. Product clarity makes my service tangible with a defined outcome. And subsequently, I can now charge more for it because it's a 'promise' of an outcome that I am making to my clients instead of just golf lessons.

# CHAPTER 10: PIXIE DUST

Three months had passed since I completed my course of lessons with David and business had gone from strength to strength. I was consistently selling 8-10 products per month and been able to restrict my working hours down to a maximum of five days a week – although it still included the odd Saturday. I was even considering putting my prices up.

The Hibbert household had taken on a regular status of calm, the kids seemed settled and happy, and Susan had a distinct glow about her. She was sat at the kitchen table pouring over the contracts for the mortgage company; we were looking at moving house. Somewhere slightly closer to the new course I was now based at on the far side of Oxford.

I was busying myself making coffee, preparing Weetabix for the kids and jam on toast for Susan.

My phone rang! Susan shot me a look. We had a rule about not using technology during mealtimes.

"It's an old client, Simon, do you mind, darling?" I asked.

"No! Go on, take it, I'll sort breakfast out." Reluctantly she replied as I walked out of the kitchen into the hallway.

"Simon, how the devil are you? How's your game coming along…"

------

I came back into the kitchen.

"Which Simon was that?" Susan inquired, "Stu's work buddy?"

"Yes, darling. Very exciting actually. Do you remember he

booked my 'drive 30 yards further' course back in November?"
Susan nodded at me, "Well, he's just asked if he can book another
course; the 'lower your handicap by ten course'. It's amazing. No
sales on my part, he just said, how can I pay and when can I start?
Isn't that amazing?"

I reached for my phone again.

"Darling!! Put it away." Susan said sternly.

"I just need to text David; he'll be thrilled. I can't believe it." I was
bounding around the room like a young puppy chasing a ball.

David didn't take the time to reply in his usual manner, which
was to make me sweat it out for a few hours before receiving a text
back. To my surprise, he called me back immediately.

"Russ! That's fantastic news. That's what I call 'The Pixie Dust'.
Even I hadn't predicted that clients might want to complete more

than one of your courses. It does make perfect sense
though, doesn't it? You gave Simon exactly the result
you'd promised, and hey presto that's one customer-
for-life created right there." David seemed as excited
as I did.

As I spoke to David my phone went ping with another message.
I glanced down at it. "Ha! David, I just got another message. It's
from Simon; he paid already."

"That's amazing Russ; I'm so happy for you. I meant to touch
base and see how you were anyway, so this is great timing. Fancy
grabbing a coffee next week? It's on me. I'd love to catch up and
see how things have gone in the last few months for you."

"I'm at the course much of next week but how about you swing by on Thursday or Friday and we'll swing a few clubs and then grab some lunch afterwards? Oh, and I'm at the new course now by the way. Richard and I had a minor…disagreement. It seems we had differing views on how to make his course work. Anyway, I'm at the new course now!"

David agreed, and we put a date in the diary for the following Friday.

------

A thunderstorm raged around the new course as we sought shelter in the refuge of the clubhouse. Luckily, we'd managed to get a full 50 minutes practice in before the heavens opened. The storm seemed ominously close as there was no gap between the flashes of lightning and bolts of thunder.

"I don't know about you, Russ, but I'm starving. What do you recommend?" David seemed oblivious to the chaos happening outside. The wind and rain were whipping around, debris being thrown across the course, lightning filling the darkened sky. As we walked to the bar, Kerry answered David's question for me, "Hey, Russ! Wild boar chilli with bubble and squeak, washed down with a pint of pale ale?" The question was rhetorical as Kerry was already writing it down on the ticket.

"Make that two," David announced.

We sat down near the window, me somewhat nervously given the proximity to the storm outside.

"So, it sounds like things are going great guns, Russ? Cheers!" We chinked pint glasses, "The new office is pretty swanky too, Russ. A good move."

"I know, I'm so glad to be away from that idiot, Richard. The less said, the better. But, no, things have been great since moving to the new course. I've a great set of regular clients, but the guy booking the second course; now that surprised me."

"I call it the 'pixie dust' when something unexpected like that happens – the repeat business. Even I didn't predict that." He said incredulously, "But it makes perfect sense. You've nailed the product, pricing and value proposition. Creating a long term Customer Lifetime Value as you have is simple, obvious and yet sometimes so easy to miss."

"Customer lifetime value?" I quizzed David for more.

**David's Lesson on Customer Lifetime Value**

David smiled and wrote down two numbers on a piece of paper.

£10,000

£1,000

"Which of these numbers is bigger?" he asked.

"Well, £10,000 obviously!" I smirked, knowing full well that it was a trick question.

Obviously. However, you can look at it slightly differently. I worked with a creative agency last year who specialised in building websites. They've been in business for ten years and, when they first started out, were encouraged by their mentors to deliver five and six-figure projects. Recently they launched one £10,000 project and some smaller £1,000 projects. It wasn't quite ten but to make the sums easier let's assume it was ten. So, look at these two numbers:

1 x £10,000

10 x £1,000

Now the two numbers are equal. Through questioning my client further, I discovered they have a fixed £50 per month support and hosting charge regardless of the size of the project. Now, it took little extra work to build a single £10k website to building ten smaller websites. However, when you start to factor in the monthly retained income the numbers look incredibly different, for example over 1 year:

1 x £10,000 + £50 per month = £10,600

But...

10 x £1,000 + 10 x £50 per month = £16,000

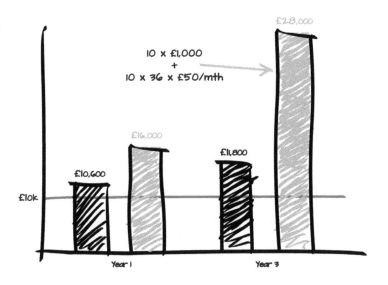

Typically their clients are loyal and stay with them for three years or more. By the end of year one, those ten smaller contracts are worth 50% more than the single five-figure project. By the end of year three, those smaller contracts are worth a whopping 275% more than the single figure project.

Too many business owners nowadays, in my opinion, focus heavily on the initial sale and completely forget about creating loyalty with their customers. It's the loyal customers, the raving fans, who are the ones who come back and do two things. Firstly, they buy from you time and time again. Secondly, they are your best form of marketing. They will refer you to their friends without even thinking about it, providing you deliver whatever you promise them.

Now, you might not have a 'support' package, but you've created repeat business which is much more valuable.

The added benefit is that it creates steady cash flow. While my client was busy chasing the bigger projects, they soon came to realise that this created boom and bust periods. Sometimes it would be months, even years between taking deposits for large development projects and collecting the final payment upon collection. The smaller jobs not only increased cash flow but consistently introduced support fees into the business. They take cash up front for smaller projects, and support fees are paid by direct debit on the first of every month. The support fees directly cover their overheads, direct costs and staff.

For you, the next step might be to introduce a support package or top-up feature. Maybe, your clients pay £595 for the initial eight-week course; could you then sign your clients up to a £50-£100 per month membership? Through membership, your clients can access competitions, reduced green fees, discounts on equipment and merchandise, and discounts off further lessons. You could run regular question and answer webinars and deliver videos on the latest golf trends and tips.

------

As usual, David was annoyingly right and incredibly inspiring. Several people have asked about how they contact me after their course had finished. A subscription program seemed like a natural follow on.

"Also, Russ, I might have an opportunity for you. You remember that 'Little Black Book' I mentioned. Well, a colleague is putting on a conference for sports professionals in Arizona. They've asked me to speak, but, I'd like you to tell your story. If you're up for it of course?" he could see the cogs were whirring in my head, "Flights, and hotel all paid for, who knows I might be able to wangle getting Susan and the kids along too."

"Are you serious? Yes! Yes, of course, David, that would be amazing." Then it dawned on me, "How big is the conference? How many people will be there?"

"Well, only about 3,500 or so."

"WHAAAT?! The most people I've spoken in front of is 40 at my wedding. I was so nervous that had I managed to spill my drink everywhere."

"Don't worry; I know a guy. He's called the 'Presentation Maestro'. I'll introduce you to Michael, he's brilliant and will get you ready for the talk. You'll be fine." David lifted his glass again, "Cheers!"

# CHAPTER 11: FREEDOM

I looked across to Susan. I smiled. She smiled back. Jacob was asleep on Susan's lap, and Elena was fast asleep in her seat. The stewardess walked over and laid a British Airways blanket over Elena.

We were somewhere over the Atlantic Ocean, at about 36,000 feet. The hum of the engines roared as I turned and gazed out at the clouds beneath us.

In the run-up to the event, I'd panicked about going away for two weeks which would have an immediate impact on my lessons. I'd run this concern by David, and he said, "Hire someone!"

So, I did. A young 19-year-old buck who had a sublime swing and plenty of swagger, but also enough maturity to take on the five products I'd produced. He picked up the sales and delivery processes in quick smart time; and, while he wasn't me, I just said to myself, "What's the worst that could happen?" Susan, the kids and I needed a break. I grabbed it with both hands.

Ever true to his word, David had managed to get me the gig to speak at the conference. I'd seized the opportunity and asked if I could bring the family. They said yes. David even asked if the conference organisers would mind flying us all out on business class. And they agreed. We were flying straight into Arizona, where David was due to meet us off the plane. Staying there for four nights and then heading on to Florida for ten nights, Juno Beach to be precise.

Somehow David had arranged for me to stay in Jarrett Park's condo. Jarrett was the organiser of the conference I was to be speaking at, and he'd offered, not only his condo to me for the duration of our stay, but also his membership pass to the Seminole Golf Club.

------

I looked out at 3,500 eager conference goers as I walked up onto the stage. They audience were applauding. I remembered Michael's first piece of advice. Take three deep breaths, right down into your belly before you speak. I did this when I'd stopped, and the applause was dying down.

I realised that I was clutching the presentation pointer in my right hand, and the lectern in my left hand. Michael's second piece of advice; don't hide behind props, use them.

The whole experience was proving to be incredibly surreal.

Michael's tip number three; remember this is not about you, it's about your audience. If you're nervous and thinking about yourself, you're not going to deliver a brilliant talk. You lose, the audience lose. It's not about you; it's about your audience. They've got your back. They want you to succeed in delivering the best talk of your life.

I walked round in front of the lectern. I turned and looked at a picture of myself, standing tall overlooking a par 3, filling up a 20-foot tall projector screen.

"Imagine every day struggling with your business, lacking confidence, not being able to put food on the table. Well, that was me nine months ago; I was a struggling golf professional. Clients weren't showing up to lessons, and I was losing money as a result of it. If that's you, well I'm going to help change all of that today during my talk, and by the end of it, you'll know how to grow and turn your business around within the next three months just like

I did. For those who I haven't had the pleasure of meeting yet, my name is Russell Hibbert…"

------

Precisely 57 minutes later people in the audience were on their feet, applauding. I couldn't believe it. What a feeling. I raised my hand and waved, and nodded a thank you to the audience before making my way off stage.

David greeted me at the side of the room, shook my hand, placing his other on my shoulder with a loud, resounding, "Well done, Russ, you smashed it. I knew you would. Hey, Jarrett, come here, I want to introduce you to Russell."

Jarrett Parks came over, "It's a pleasure to meet you, Russell."

"A pleasure to meet you too – I love your latest book, Jarrett, I read it cover to cover on the flight over," I replied, pumping with adrenaline.

"Any time you want to speak at one of my events again, Russ, you'd be more than welcome." Jarrett let go of his iron grip on my hand, "By the way, what's your offer?"

"My offer?" I was confused, had I missed something.

"Yeah, you didn't give your offer out at the end of your talk. Everyone has an offer, like, what next?" Jarrett said. I kicked myself. David immediately saw my restlessness and came to my rescue.

"Ah, that's my fault, I was meant to ask you on Russell's behalf. Russell's wife doesn't play golf, and he was wondering whether his offer could be a five days lessons and a chance to play at Seminole as Russ's guest."

I looked bemused at David, not fully understanding what was happening. David just looked at me with a huge smile and winked.

"Of course, yes, David my old friend, yes." Jarrett started making his way towards the stage. He ushered the crowd to quieten down and made an announcement.

"In Russell's haste to deliver such great value during his talk, which he did, right?" The crowd cheered, "He forgot to let you know about his current, fantastic offer. Russell is staying out in his condo in Seminole this week…"

"My condo?" I thought.

Susan came up to me, slid her hand into mine, and whispered in my ear, "Well done darling, you crushed it, I'm so proud of you."

Jarrett continued, "…and he's got five spaces free for one-to-one lessons followed by the opportunity to play a round of golf at Seminole, with Russell himself. If you want to know more, please go to my stand at the back of the room, and ask for my assistant Jennifer. It's first come, first served folks. Now, your next speaker needs no introduction, my protégé; please give a warm Arizona welcome to The Business Wizard, David Marchant."

To my astonishment, at least a dozen people stood up from their chairs and started jostling to get to the back of the room while the rest of the audience applauded David onto the stage. Jarrett shook David's hand as he passed David on the stage and then made his way back to me.

"My condo?" I asked.

Jarrett smiled at me, "Well, it will be for the next ten days, Russ. So, make the most of it. You're full by the looks of it." He pointed at the back of the room to Jennifer, who was waving and giving a two thumbs up. "Go and have a chat with Jenni, she'll sort you out from here. We've got another event in the Hamptons in 3 months; I'd love for you to speak on that one."

Still, in a daze, Susan and I made our way down the side of the auditorium to Jennifer. I was stopped several times en route by people grabbing my hand to shake it, telling me what a great talk I'd given.

My phone buzzed, I looked down. Richard. I hit cancel and smiled to myself. No more having to deal with that idiot, I thought to myself.

Jennifer rushed over to greet us, "All five spaces, gone Russell. Great job. I need to sort out the payment for you if that's ok?"

"Payment?"

"Yes, $50,000." She smiled.

"$50,000?"

"You sold out, five lessons and a crack at Seminole. $10,000 for each space. So, $50,000." She fired up her MacBook and logged into First National Bank, "Do you know your IBAN and Swift?" she asked.

 Susan was already a step ahead and had logged into my business bank account for me. She lay her phone down in front of Jennifer so she could read the account details. I looked at Susan. "$50,000?" I said, again. Finally, I felt like I was no longer drifting and had a strong sense of purpose.

# CHAPTER 12: SUNSET

There is nothing more beautiful than being able to enjoy a sunset, with a mojito in hand and enjoying the peace of nature bequeathed by some of the best golf courses around the world.

In this instance, I am sat on the terrace of the clubhouse at the Bali National Golf Course waiting for my first students to arrive.

Just then Susan walks past the terrace just below where I'm sitting. She looks beautiful in a flowing white summer dress, which is being caught in the breeze. There's a flurry of movement and giggles as Elena shoots past Susan, with Jacob in hot pursuit. Well, as fast as a near 2-year-old can go at least. Shortly afterwards, Jacob takes a nose-dive into the bunker just off the 18th. They're all laughing hysterically at this point, even Jacob as he wipes the sand from his face.

Susan looks over to me with a broad smile and beckons me to come and join them.

I take a few moment to capture the scene and then push off from the post of the veranda which I had been leaning.

------

Shortly after Arizona, and Seminole, David helped me set up The Golf Pro Academy. The GPA is now my signature retreat for entrepreneurial Golf Professionals where, once a quarter, I run week-long retreats for 10-20 pros to exotic courses around the world. The week typically involves teaching my students the basics of running a lifestyle business, playing golf and enjoying life.

I get to choose which course they will be held at and at what times of the year I want to go. It's not a fortune, but my profit after expenses is in the region of £250k which is plenty to go towards helping to achieve the goals the Susan and I originally wrote down.

It still amazes me that two years ago, I was thinking about giving up on my dream of being a golf professional and being able to teach others the sport that I love.

There's another small bonus as well.

I've just purchased a plot of land next door to the range in Oxfordshire and the local council have approved a Golf Academy. I intend to run week long golf camps for inner city children who would otherwise never get the opportunity to pick up a club or spend time in the open countryside.

The council offered to match fund the project, but I asked instead for them to make a donation to charity. For every child who undertakes our programme for a day, they will fund a sports program for a child in India via Buy1Give1. That means that for the princely sum of £0.21 a child somewhere else in the world benefits from playing the sport. For every one person who signs up to one of my retreats, ten children can complete a sports program for a year.

As I walk down to Susan and the children, I think back over the last two years. About how lucky I was to meet David when I did. How he helped me to determine my goals. When he showed me that I needed a strong desire to overcome all of the challenges that were to stand in my way. And most importantly the activities I now need to do to realise my goals. Most of all I can't believe how lucky I am. And I wonder for a moment, "What's next? What will *My Next Shot* entail?"

# NEXT STEPS

There are a number of ways to take your next steps after reading this book, first and foremost check out Robin's website for his latest updates, events, and The Fearless Business Coaching Programme:

http://robinwaite.com

You can also email Robin personally at robin@robinwaite.com with any questions you might have about Take Your Shot.

It is essential if this book has inspired you even a little bit, to take action in your business. My goal for the book was to help to change the perceptions of your own business and to start the journey of change with your business. Because let's face it, nothing is going to change if you keep on doing the same old thing.

*** REVIEW OFFER ***

If you feel this book would help someone else, I would like to invite you to leave a review on Amazon to help spread the word about Take Your Shot.

If you leave a review of Take Your Shot and send me a screenshot or link to your review, I would like to offer you a FREE 60-minute consultation to help you Take Your Shot with your own business.

I've helped business owners double and treble their income, and I would love the opportunity to be able to help you do that too.

But, most of all, thank you for taking the time to read Take Your Shot. If I've even initiated the smallest light bulb moment in you, I have achieved my goal with the book.

**92** TAKE YOUR SHOT

# ABOUT THE AUTHOR

The first job I took was a paper round, the longest one in the village I lived in, and it paid the most amount of money. The tips I collected every Christmas for four years were bigger than any of the other delivery boys and girls. It meant I could afford to buy two or three CDs a week whereas most of my peers struggled to afford one or two per month.

Soon I was investing my paper-round money in second-hand CDs and selling them at my school to my peers so that I could afford the latest albums and the best Sony hi-fi I could afford.

Not knowing what business I wanted to start; at 18 I worked as a systems analyst, which gave me an enormous insight into systems and processes but my methods resulted in staff in the company I worked at being made redundant. The money wasn't great, so by 22, I'd started a great sideline selling grade-B laptops. I made enough money to quit my job and, in one summer, made over £40,000. Mostly cash (declared, I might add) but that money was sat on the end of my bed. I did what any savvy 22-year-old would have done and bought a car, and booked a holiday with my girlfriend to Florida to see her brother.

While out in Florida I got a call from an old colleague to start up a creative agency.

My design agency wasn't like any other; ordinarily, a new client would submit a request-for-quote, which would trigger this game of "design agency ping-pong." This involved months of back and forth between the agency and customer. I knew there had to be a better way than doing everything remotely; so I created a series of intensive 1-to-1 workshops.

The workshops involved the client working directly with a strategy expert and either a developer or designer – depending on whether it was a website or branding workshop. Typically, this would take 1-2 days.

Logo design, for example; is a process which can take up to eight weeks to create a professional logo. This lengthy process is down to poor communication or lack of time. We charged £60 per hour, and a logo might generate 8-10 hours of chargeable work during that eight-week game of design agency ping-pong.

I invited the client in for a one-to-one, 1-day branding workshop. The process had seven steps with clearly defined outcomes. We charged a fixed price which was £1,495, nearly three times the hourly rate previously charged. I offered a 100% money back guarantee. I did the same with websites and created a 2-day prototyping workshop. It started to slot into place.

Four years later.

After speeding down Frocester Hill at 50+ mph, I split off from my cycling club buddies and found myself stood next to a railway line. All I could think was, "I want more, I want to go faster!" A train whooshed past. My thoughts turned to, "What if I had stood in front of that train?" quickly countered by, "Well, I wasn't! So, something had to change." – I realised that something was missing in my life and I had to act.

After talking things through with my life coach, Michael Serwa, we realised that I wasn't passionate about building websites or designing logos, I had created a "job" for myself. However, I loved working with people, teaching them, creating products for them, building assets, and creating systems so they could charge more.

Michael said to me during one session, "Robin, it sounds to me like you're coaching!"

I spent three months rebranding and relaunched myself as a business coach. I had set a goal. I wanted to get ten clients within my first year. I created 14 clients in 6 weeks. At the age of 35 I am now running a 6-figure coaching business with great clients, and it is thanks to Michael, my coach, for kicking me into action and giving me the belief that I could do it.

Now, I coach other businesses owners and managers to do what I did. My niche is professional service businesses. From creative agencies turning over £20k+ per year to large accountancy firms turning over £2m+. I have created a number of my coaching tools to facilitate my fortnightly or monthly meetings with my clients.

I get a tremendous sense of achievement when I see my clients' businesses prosper and I have a goal to help 10,000 business owners in the next five years to double their turnover within six months using my tools. I can't do this all on a one-to-one basis, so I have created a number of coaching tools and programmes, and deliver regular talks and workshops to enable me to achieve my goal.

http://robinwaite.com

# FEARLESS BUSINESS

Fearless Business is for anyone who is serious about growing their business, and potentially doubling your turnover and profit within the next 6 months.

But...you will become part of a family where I am the mother hen - I am incredibly proud of my brood whenever they have amazing wins, and lightbulb moments!!!

There are a number of things you will get access to:

- Weekly 2 Hour Webinar Panel Q&A
- Access to Discounted Breakthrough Sessions
- The Fearless Business Course (worth £195)
- The 7-Day Fearless Challenges (worth £95 each) once per month
- Accountability in the Fearless Business Group
- Message me anytime you like (don't take the p*ss) with you challenges and I'll jump on it ASAP.
- Online Business Startup Course (worth £30)
- Copies of Online Business Startup and pre-release copies of my next two books, before anyone else.
- Access to my little black book of contacts

You can apply to join at any time.

Fearless Business is ONLY £125/mth. And by application ONLY:

http://robinwaite.com/fearless/application/

That's priority access to me for only £125/mth which is an absolute bargain IMHO.

Interested??? Get online and apply.

# READING LIST

| Title | What It'sAbout |
|---|---|
| **Think and Grow Rich** Napoleon Hill | We can learn to think like the rich we can discover wealth and success. |
| **Built to Sell** John Warrilow | Creating a Business That Can Thrive Without You |
| **Go For No** Richard Fenton and Andrea Waltz | Yes is the Destination, No is How You Get There |
| **The Startup Coach** Carl Reader | Other books help you talk the talk; the Teach Yourself Coach books will help you walk the walk. |
| **The Lean Startup** Eric Reis | How Today's Entrepreneurs Use Continuous Innovation to Create Radically Successful Businesses |
| **The Prosperous Coach** Steve Chandler and Rich Litvin | Increase Income and Impact for You and Your Clients |
| **How to Be F\*cking Awesome** Dan Meredith | A kick up the backside to finally launch that business, start a new project you've been putting off or just become all round awesome. |
| **24 Assets** Daniel Priestley | Create a digital, scalable, valuable and fun business that will thrive in a fast changing world |
| **The Phoenix Project** Gene Kim and Kevin Behr | A Novel About IT, DevOps, and Helping Your Business Win |
| **Principled Selling** David Tovey | How to Win More Business Without Selling Your Soul |

| Title | What It's About |
|---|---|
| **Elon Musk**<br>Ashlee Vance | How the Billionaire CEO of SpaceX and Tesla is Shaping our Future |
| **From Good to Amazing**<br>Michael Serwa | No Bullshit Tips for The Life You Always Wanted |
| **The Goal**<br>Jeff Cox, Eliyahu Goldratt | A Process of Ongoing Improvement |
| **The Big Leap**<br>Gay Hedricks | Conquer Your Hidden Fear and Take Life to the Next Level |
| **Sell or Be Sold**<br>Grant Cardone | How to Get Your Way in Business and Life |
| **Flash Boys**<br>Michael Lewis | If you thought Wall Street was about alpha males standing in trading pits hollering at each other, think again |
| **Life Leverage**<br>Rob Moore | How to Get More Done in Less Time, Outsource Everything & Create Your Ideal Mobile Lifestyle |
| **Online Business Startup**<br>Robin Waite | The entrepreneur's guide to launching a fast, lean and profitable online venture |
| **Outliers**<br>Malcolm Gladwell | The Story of Success |